# My Holiday in
# South Africa

## Jane Bingham

Published in paperback in 2014 by Wayland
Copyright © Wayland 2014

Wayland
338 Euston Road
London NW1 3BH

Wayland Australia
Level 17/207 Kent Street
Sydney NSW 2000

Produced for Wayland by

White Thomson Publishing Ltd
www.wtpub.co.uk
+44 (0)843 2087 460

Senior Editor: Victoria Brooker
Editors: Jane Bingham/Steve White-Thomson
Designer: Ian Winton
Map artwork: Stefan Chabluk
Proofreader: Alice Harman

British Library Cataloguing in Publication Data
Bingham, Jane
  My holiday in South Africa
  1. Vacations – South Africa – Juvenile literature
  2. South Africa – Juvenile literature
  I. Title II. South Africa
  916.8'0468

  ISBN 978 0 7502 8313 7

Wayland is a division of Hachette Children's Books,
an Hachette UK company.

Printed in China

10 9 8 7 6 5 4 3 2 1

Cover: Ndebele woman: Dreamstime/Temistocle Lucarelli;
Capetown: Shutterstock/michaeljung.

p.1: Dreamstime/Inna Felker; p.5: Shutterstock/urosr;
p.6: Dreamstime/Alexandre Fagundes De Fagundes;
p.7: Shutterstock/Luisa Puccini; p.8: Dreamstime/
Hongqi Zhang; p.9: Shutterstock/PhotoSky 4t com;
p.10: Shutterstock/Dominique de La Croix; p.11
(top): Dreamstime/Martin Applegate;  p.11 (middle):
Dreamstime/Luke Schmidt; p.11 (bottom): Shutterstock/
peppi18; p.12: Shutterstock/michaeljung; p.13:
Wikipedia/Vberger; p.14: Shutterstock/Luke Schmidt;
p.15(top): Shutterstock/Richard Cavalieri; p.15 (bottom)
Shutterstock/catwalker; p.16 (top): Shutterstock/
Sean Nel; p.16 (bottom): Dreamstime /Dandamanwasch;
p.17: Shutterstock/J Reineke; p.18: Dreamstime /Nico
Smit; p.19: Shutterstock/wcpmedia; p.20: Dreamstime /
Temistocle Lucarelli; p.21: Shutterstock/michaeljung;
p.22: Dreamstime /Villiers Steyn; p.23: Shutterstock/
Four Oaks; p.24: Dreamstime /Anke Van Wyk; p.25:
Shutterstock/Eva Gruendemann; p.26 (top): Dreamstime
/Maxirf; p.26 (bottom): Shutterstock/oconnelll;
p.27: Dreamstime /Inna Felker; p.28: Shutterstock/
Peter Wollinga; p.29: Shutterstock/fstockfoto; p.30:
Shutterstock/Nicole Gordine.

# Contents

This is South Africa! 4

Warm and sunny 6

Somewhere to stay 8

Travelling around 10

Wonderful Cape Town 12

Cities and towns 14

On the coast 16

Mountains and caves 18

Meeting people 20

On safari 22

Time to eat 24

Let's go shopping! 26

Sports and games 28

Make it yourself 30

Useful words 32

# This is South Africa!

South Africa is a large country on the southern tip of the **continent** of Africa. Most people travel there by aeroplane.

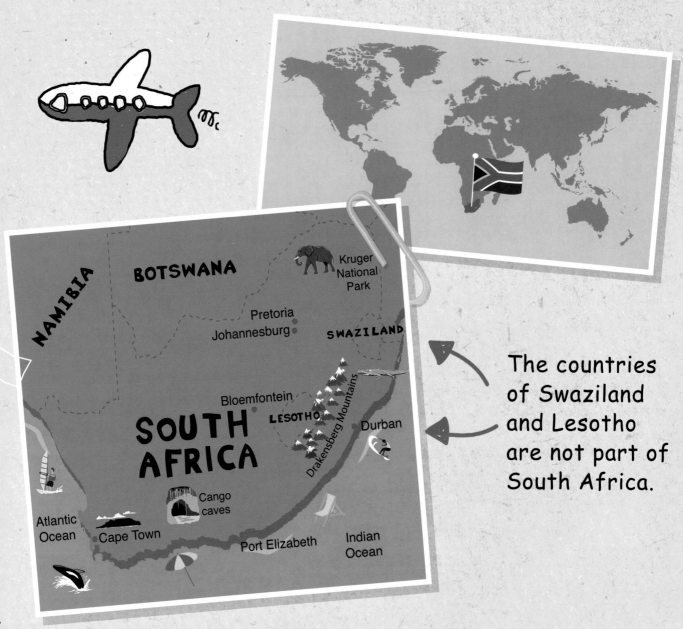

The countries of Swaziland and Lesotho are not part of South Africa.

This man is taking bananas to sell in a market.

Arriving in South Africa feels very exciting. Everywhere you look there are surprising sights.

I felt tired after the flight, but it was amazing to be in Africa.

## South African words

**hello**
howzit

**nice**
lekker

**countryside**
veldt

# Warm and sunny

The weather in South Africa is usually warm and sunny. But you need to be prepared for sudden showers.

It is warm on the coast and cooler in the mountains.

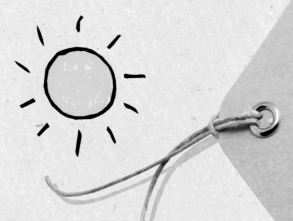

## Don't forget to pack

- sun hat
- swimming costume
- warm top
- raincoat

If you want to see wild animals, the best months to visit are July and August. This is winter time in South Africa. The weather is still warm, but many bushes and trees are bare so it is easier to spot the animals.

These people are watching zebras in a **national park**.

# Somewhere to stay

Visitors to South Africa often stay in a hotel or a **guest house**.

Durban has big hotels along the seafront.

Guest houses are usually run by **Afrikaans** families. The Afrikaans language sounds like Dutch.

## Speak Afrikaans!

**please**
asseblief (ass-er-**bleef**)

**thank you**
dankie (**dun**-key)

**yes**
ja (yah)

Inside the national parks there are rest camps where you can stay the night.

The rest camps have small houses called chalets. Each chalet is large enough for a family.

Our chalet was really cosy, and we made friends with the children staying next door.

# Travelling around

South Africa has fantastic beaches, mountains, forests and deserts. It's good to travel around and see as much of the country as you can.

Fast trains run between the cities. This train is passing a beach near Cape Town.

Visitors often hire a car and drive themselves around. You see some interesting sights when you travel by road.

Some children waved to us on their way to school.

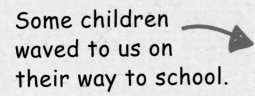

We saw small houses in villages.

One day we surprised a family of giraffes!

# Wonderful Cape Town

The city of Cape Town lies between the mountains and the sea. Behind the city is Table Mountain with its long, flat top.

A cable car takes visitors up Table Mountain. The view from the top is amazing.

There are so many fun things to do in Cape Town! Some people head for the shops and some visit museums. There are also lots of places to see animals.

You get a really close-up view in the Two Oceans Aquarium!

## Cape Town treats

**See the Kids' Show** – at the Planetarium

**Swim in a huge rock pool** – at Sea Point Pavillion

**Try hands-on activities** – at the MTN Science Centre

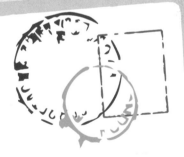

# Cities and towns

South Africa has three capital cities. The president lives in Pretoria, **parliament** meets in Cape Town and the law courts are in Bloemfontein.

Johannesburg is South Africa's biggest city. The final of the Football World Cup was played there in 2010.

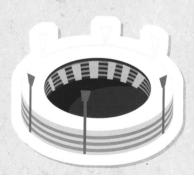

Soweto is close to Johannesburg. It is a very poor area. Nelson Mandela lived there when he was a young man.

The houses in Soweto are made from anything people can find.

President
Nelson R
Mandela

SOUTH AFRICA
SUID-AFRIKA 45c
Ab1.4
1994

Mandela led the movement to end unfair treatment of black South Africans. Today, all South Africans have equal rights.

15

# On the coast

South Africa has some wonderful sandy beaches. They are perfect for swimming and water sports.

Kiteboarders love the long, flat beaches close to Durban.

People go windsurfing on the southern coast, around Cape Town.

The iSimangaliso Wetland Park is a long stretch of **swampy** land along the east coast. It is a great place to watch crocodiles, hippos, turtles and pelicans.

This hippo and her babies are enjoying the water in the Wetland Park.

## Coastal creatures to spot:

seals      whales

dolphins      turtles

penguins      sharks

# Mountains and caves

Parts of South Africa are very wild and rocky. There are stunning mountains and caves to explore.

You can take a tour of the Cango caves. Long pillars of rock, called stalactites, hang down from the roofs of the caves.

It felt dark and spooky inside the Cango caves!

The Drakensberg Mountains run along the eastern side of South Africa. People have been living in caves in these mountains for over 30,000 years.

Many cave paintings have been found in the mountains. Some of them were painted thousands of years ago.

This cave painting shows people and animals. The animals are probably **antelopes**.

# Meeting people

There are many different African peoples living in South Africa. One of the largest groups is the Ndebele (Oon-de-**beh**-lay).

Some Ndebele people still have a **traditional** way of life. They dress in bold colours and decorate their houses with striking patterns.

Many South Africans are **descended** from **settlers**. In the past, settlers arrived from Holland, Britain, India and Malaysia. Their descendants all became South Africans.

South Africa is sometimes called the rainbow nation because its people belong to many different races.

# On safari

Many visitors to South Africa go on safari. You ride through a national park with an expert guide to point out the animals.

If you are lucky, you will see lions, elephants, leopards, rhinos and buffalo on safari. These animals are known as 'the big five'.

## Other animals to spot on safari:

- giraffes
- zebras
- cheetahs
- antelopes

22

The national parks provide a safe place for animals to live.

These elephants live in an elephant sanctuary, where they are protected from **hunters**.

# Be prepared on safari

- Wear dull colours so the animals can't spot you.
- Don't forget binoculars and a camera.

# Time to eat

People in South Africa love to eat meat! They often cook their meat on a barbecue, called a braai (bry).

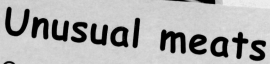

These long, spicy sausages are called boerewors (**boo**-ruh-vors).

## Unusual meats

On your holiday, you may be offered emu, ostrich or even crocodile meat!

Be prepared to try some surprising mixtures. This curry is made from bananas, peanuts, dried fruits and kidney beans.

## On the menu

**biltong** (**bil**-tong)
strips of dried meat

**sosatie** (sos-**ar**-tee)
barbecued meat on skewers, with apricots and a curry sauce

**koeksister** (**cook**-sis-ter)
a plaited doughnut soaked in sticky syrup

# Let's go shopping!

South Africa has all kinds of shops. In the big cities, there are modern shopping centres and large open-air markets.

This shopping centre is in Pretoria.

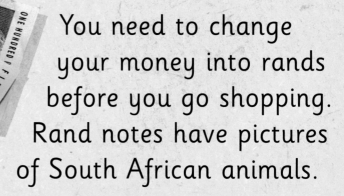

You need to change your money into rands before you go shopping. Rand notes have pictures of South African animals.

In the countryside, you will sometimes see people by the side of the road selling things they have made.

These Ndebele women are selling dolls and jewellery.

# Sports and games

If you enjoy outdoor activities, South Africa is the place for you! You can try exciting water sports such as sailing, surfing and **kayaking**, and there are lots of chances to go hiking and horse riding.

Pony trekking is a great way to enjoy the countryside.

South Africans love rugby, football and cricket. When South Africa hosted the Football World Cup, the crowds went wild!

Football supporters blow a kind of trumpet, called a vuvuzela.

I went to a football match. It was very exciting but the vuvuzelas were really noisy!

# Make it yourself

You can make a colourful picture frame decorated with Ndebele patterns. It will make the perfect frame for a postcard of South Africa!

Use colourful patterns like the ones on these bracelets.

**You will need:**

- 1 sheet of thick paper, A4 size
- ruler
- pencil
- scissors
- felt-tip pens
- glue
- postcard

## Step 1

Fold the paper in half. Place your postcard in the centre of one side of the folded paper and draw around it.

**Rectangle (a)**

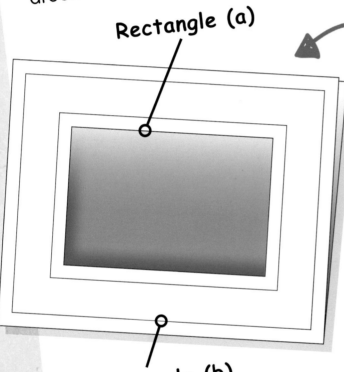

**Rectangle (b)**

## Step 2

Remove the card and draw two more rectangles. Draw rectangle (a) 5 mm inside your first rectangle. Draw rectangle (b) 15 mm outside your first rectangle. Cut along the lines of rectangle (a) to make a window for your picture.

## Step 3

Decorate your frame using colourful Ndebele patterns. Glue the sides of the frame together, leaving the top open. Now slide your postcard into your picture frame!

# Useful words

| | |
|---|---|
| **Afrikaans** | South Africans who are descended from Dutch settlers. |
| **antelope** | An animal with horns, that looks rather like a deer and runs very fast. |
| **continent** | One of seven large areas of land on the Earth. The seven continents are Africa, Antarctica, Asia, Australia, Europe, North America and South America. |
| **descended** | Coming from a group of people with a long history. |
| **hunter** | Someone who hunts and kills animals. |
| **guest house** | A small hotel, usually run by a family. |
| **kayaking** | A water sport in which you paddle a small canoe, called a kayak. |
| **national park** | A large area of wild land that people can visit. Animals in national parks are kept safe from harm. |
| **Ndebele** | One of the largest groups of native African people who live in South Africa. |
| **parliament** | A group of people who have been chosen to run a country. |
| **settlers** | People who travel to a different country and make their home there. |
| **swampy** | Wet and soft. |
| **traditional** | Done in the same way for many years. |